Paislee Anne

Written by: Dee Sewell

Illustrated by: Van Thang

WestBow Press books may be ordered through booksellers or by contacting:

WestBow Press
A Division of Thomas Nelson & Zondervan
1663 Liberty Drive
Bloomington, IN 47403
www.westbowpress.com
844-714-3454

Interior Image Credit: Van Thang

ISBN: 978-1-6642-3115-3 (sc)
ISBN: 978-1-6642-3117-7 (hc)
ISBN: 978-1-6642-3116-0 (e)

Library of Congress Control Number: 2021907667

Print information available on the last page.

WestBow Press rev. date: 04/27/2021

WestBow
PRESS®
A DIVISION OF THOMAS NELSON
& ZONDERVAN

To Clay and Tabitha, Paislee's parents
and all our wonderful grandchildren

Written by: Dee Sewell
Edited by: Charity Foote
Illustrated by: Van Thang

Paislee is here!

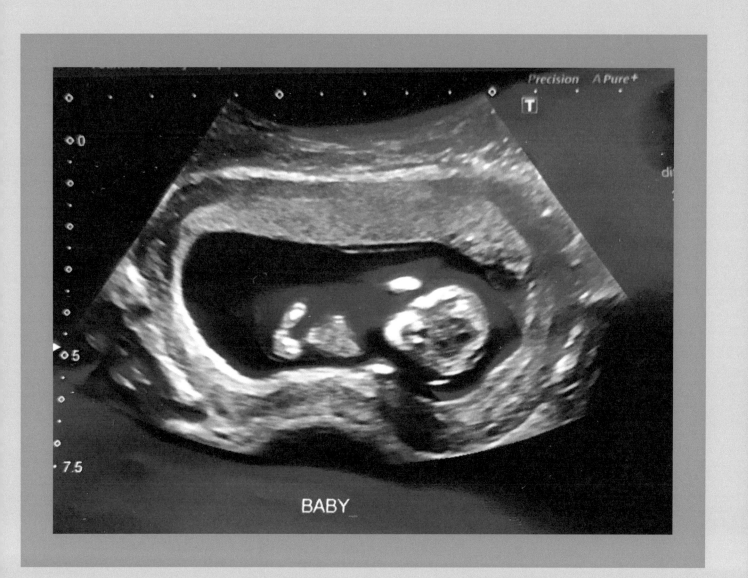

I wonder. Will Paislee like . . .

pickles, peas or peppers

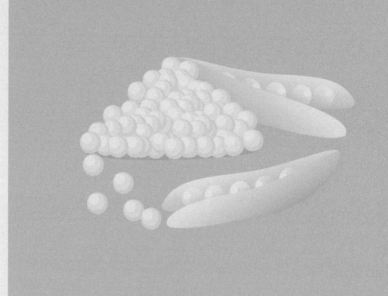

peaches, pears or persimmons

pizza, pasta or pot roast

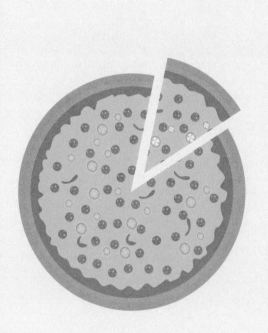

pancakes, potatoes or porridge

pretzels, peanuts or popcorn

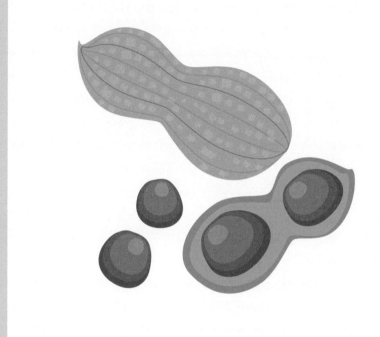

pudding, pie or popsicles

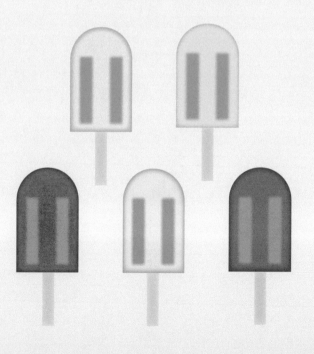

puzzles, playing cards or pin the tail on the donkey

purple, pink or periwinkle

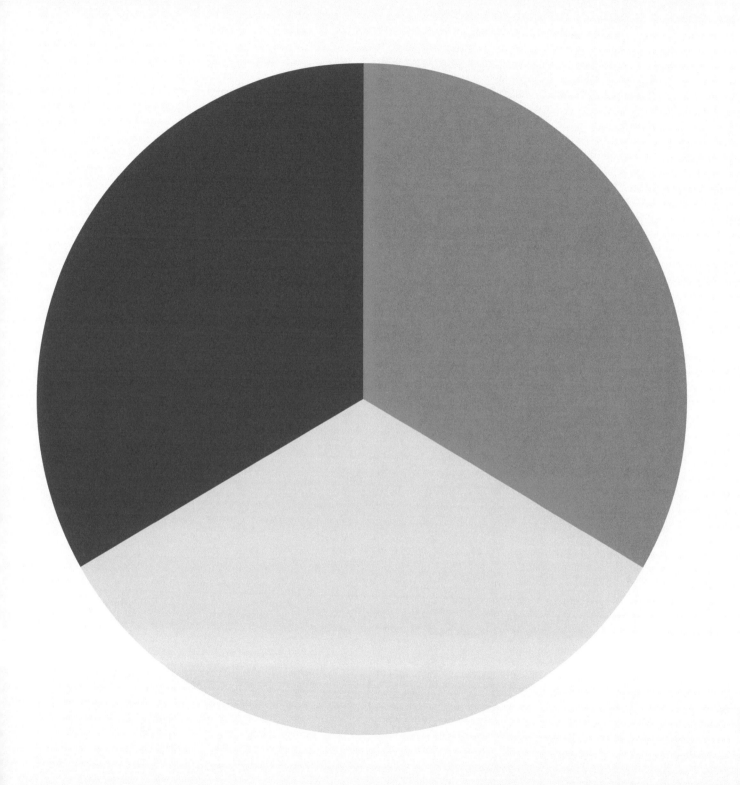

poppies, pansies or petunias

parrots, pigs or porcupines

pandas, peacocks or platypuses

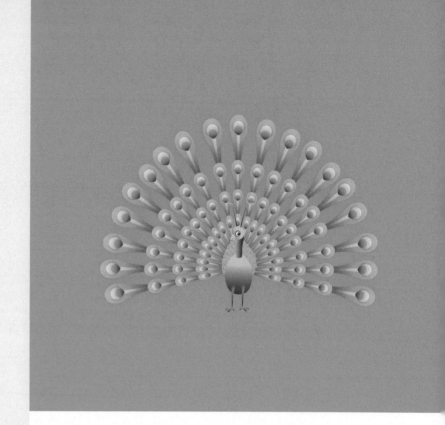

polar bears, penguins or pufferfish?

Yet I know,
what really matters the most . . .

is that Paislee knows Jesus loves her

and made her a very special person!

Printed in the United States
by Baker & Taylor Publisher Services